STARTING POINTS

Ideas for reflecting and praying together

By the same author from Geoffrey Chapman
SEARCH FOR MEANING

STARTING POINTS

Ideas for reflecting and praying together

SISTER JUDITH RUSSI

GEOFFREY
CHAPMAN

Geoffrey Chapman
an imprint of Cassell Publishers Limited
Villiers House, 41/47 Strand, London WC2N 5JE, England

First published 1991

British Library Cataloguing in Publication Data
Russi, Judith
Starting points.
1. Christian life. Meditation & prayer
I. Title
248.3

ISBN 0-225-66634-0

Typeset by Colset Private Limited, Singapore
Printed and bound in Great Britain by
Mackays of Chatham Plc

CONTENTS

ACKNOWLEDGEMENTS

Sincere thanks to Bishop James O'Brien, Bishop in Hertfordshire, for financing the piloting of these resources and for all his support and encouragement.

Grateful thanks to Brother Damian Lundy FSC and Fr Ernie Sands for their inspiration and in-service courses in the Westminster Diocese which led to many teachers asking for resources that would enable them to put into practice the vision and ideas which had been shared.

Thanks to the many Westminster teachers who have contributed their thoughts and ideas in the pilot scheme for *Starting Points*.

Thanks to the Hertfordshire area team for all their support and advice.

Thanks to the secretarial team, Helena Finn and Cecilia Finn.

Thanks to Anne King of Geoffrey Chapman, and the Nicholas Breakspear School, St Albans, for the picture on the front cover.

Biblical quotations are mostly from the Jerusalem Bible (Darton, Longman & Todd/Doubleday).

Illustrations by Cecilia Finn.

INTRODUCTION

What follows is a selection of ideas which have been well tried with teenagers and are offered to you for quiet times or periods of reflection or prayer. Although these ideas have developed mainly out of a school setting, they are just as suitable for parish-based groups and youth groups as they are in an informal educational setting. They can also be used at adult level and to provide the basis for parish liturgies. Indeed these suggestions are ideal for any situation where the aim is to create a reflective atmosphere.

Size of the group

In order to create an atmosphere which will encourage the development of reflection and prayer, these ideas are best used in a small group of say ten to thirty people. In a school, this could be a class rather than a whole year assembly and in a parish, it could be the young adults' group or part of a confirmation group.

How long should the prayer time be?

This will vary according to the amount of time available. Each of these ideas is a springboard which can be adapted to suit the needs of a particular group. Some of the ideas are quite short, others may need up to fifteen minutes, depending on the size of the group. However, quality and not quantity is the main concern. In general, though, the length of time allocated to each prayer session should be flexible and adapted to the needs and responses of the group as a whole. You may also wish to spend several prayer times on the same theme, thus deepening the theme each time.

Creating the right atmosphere

Whether in a school or a parish setting, the members of the group will have busy lives and a collective act of worship should in no way be an experience which is imposed from the top down and unrelated to the daily experience of the group. We do, however, have to recognize that there may be people, particularly in a school setting, who might be unhappy about taking part in or leading a prayer session. It is hoped that *Starting Points* offers a way into deeper thought which, if appropriate, could lead to prayer. It has to be recognized that no one can be made to pray, neither would one want to force anyone into pretending to do so.

Creating a time of quiet and calm is quickly appreciated by all involved. The sheer pace and business of each day seldom allow the community to be still together. If nothing else happens other than that there is silence in a group, then you have gone a long way on your journey to helping your group to learn how to pray.

Take time to get to know your group

This is a key principle: get to know your group, take risks carefully, know how to restore atmosphere without getting angry and thereby destroying it. Prayer is a serious time, but that shouldn't stop it being a joyful, humorous and happy occasion. You should also bear in mind the degree of commitment among the members of your group, as well as considerations such as their age, sex, race and any topical issues which may affect them. It is also important to remember that no one should feel forced to share their thoughts with the group if they don't want to, but as they all get to know each other, this should prove easier.

Leading the group

You may feel very apprehensive about leading a group as you may never have had the experience of leading people in prayer before. If this is the case, it is nothing to be afraid of, nor is there any reason to feel that you cannot do it. Praying with a small group, especially one of young people, is not only a beautiful experience, it is also very normal and natural. A point to remember is that the sincerity of the person leading the group will be one of the key factors for success.

Developing leadership from within the group

Some of these ideas require a certain amount of preparation and it is a good idea to invite a few members of the group to help you with this. This works well when the young people work with and not in place of the group leader. Results can be disastrous when the responsibility is farmed out to young people and they are left to get on with it on their own. This leads to resentment and a reluctance by the whole group to do anything.

Flexibility

This is most important. Be ready to respond to a special moment in the life of the community, be it school, a parish or wherever. For example, a major event in the lives of the young people might be a more appropriate focus of the time of prayer than the theme you had prepared. You should also be flexible in your use of this book; any ideas can be combined or adapted to suit your needs.

Focal point

Each time of prayer should have a focal point. This could be a Bible, a crucifix, a candle, a flower arrangement, an item or inspirational picture or a display relevant to the theme of the prayer session. This should be kept as simple as possible and to provide an effective focal point for the act of worship.

Where possible, encourage the members of the group to take responsibility for arranging this area themselves. It can be changed often and everyone can take their turn in the preparations for prayer and reflection.

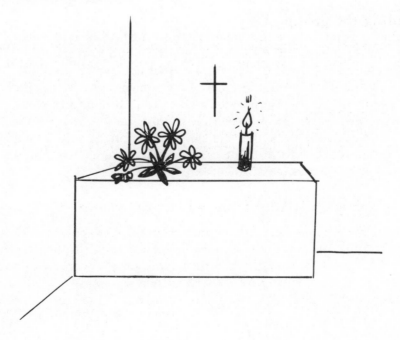

Special intentions board/box

In the daily act of worship the community strives not only to give glory to God but also to take before the Lord the lives of each individual – their joys and their sorrows. It can often be helpful to the group if they have somewhere that they can place requests for prayer. These can be incorporated into the group prayer. One or two of these can be the focus for a special prayer for the week.

Prayer journal

Keeping a prayer journal and adding thoughts, ideas, prayers and pictures daily can be a helpful aid to prayer. All that will be needed for this will be a simple notebook or exercise book for each member of the group. They should be encouraged to keep their journals as something both very special and personal. Journals could also be used when a written response is needed to a prayer/reflection starter.

Using local resources

The community (be it school or parish) may well have people with valuable backgrounds in helping people to pray. It is sometimes a good plan to invite such people to join your group in a prayer time to give their ideas and help.

Finally, it is important to remember that these ideas are designed to create an openness and attitude to reflection and prayer which will involve everyone present. They are not sit and watch sessions! Creating the right atmosphere and environment, the use of symbols and decor are all very important aids to reflection and prayer. This does not necessarily mean expensive outlay; rather, imaginative use of resources available. Often the simple re-arrangement of seating and an appropriate focal point can be far more effective than an elaborate and expensive arrangement.

WHO ARE WE?

Name prayers

YOU WILL NEED TO:

1 Provide pencils or pens and paper for each person.

2 Ensure that everyone has access to a table or something hard to lean on as they write.

3 Have your example clearly visible for everyone to see.

4 Decide with the group whether to display their name prayers. If so, you need to have a space ready in your room to save time.

5 Choose a suitable piece of music or short reading for the conclusion. However, this may not be necessary if you are going to display the group's ideas. Remember not to force anyone to share their thoughts. Everyone in the group will enjoy the session if they feel quite free to write down what they want without the fear of having their thoughts exposed.

6 If you are providing the group members with reflection/prayer books for recording their thoughts, this exercise can be entered into their books.

7 Arrange the seating in a semicircle around your focal point. When the group is seated, explain what is going to happen. This helps to settle people and ease any sense of awkwardness or embarrassment. Nothing unsettles a group more quickly than not knowing what is going on. Explain that in this time together they are being asked to reflect, to be still and, if they wish at the right moment, to share a thought or two.

Grateful thanks to Damian Lundy FSC for the idea of 'Name Prayers'.

Smile and
Understand the love you
See in
All that Jesus
Now does for you and me

or

Knowing who I
Am
Really lets me
Enjoy life
Now

▷ Show the group these two examples. You will notice that one is explicitly religious and in the other religious meaning is more implicit. This does not need pointing out but just allow the examples to stimulate the group.

▷ Ask group members to work quietly on their own. Explain that there will be time to share ideas when everyone has had a chance to think.

▷ Allow the group to illustrate or decorate their thoughts as they wish.

▷ Some of the group may be eager to share their ideas. When you feel everyone has had a chance to get their ideas down, then invite those who wish to share them to do so.

▷ When the group has completed the exercise it might be appropriate to sum up the idea with a suitable piece of music or reading, or put some of the other ideas into their journal or prayer book, e.g. Isaiah 43:1–3:

> Do not be afraid, for I have redeemed you;
> I have called you by your name, you are mine. . . .
> Should you walk through fire, you will not be scorched
> and the flames will not burn you.
> For I am Yahweh your God,
> the Holy One of Israel, your Saviour.

▶2
Using our names

YOU WILL NEED:

1 A list of the names of the people in the group in alphabetical order. Remember that this idea will take as many days as there are people in your group. It is important not to leave anyone out. If someone is missing on their day, then remember to pray for them in their absence.

It is important to let people know well in advance when their day is. Each member of the group will be free to direct the reflection/prayer time in the way that they wish.

2 A small group to prepare a notice-board or space on the wall for the daily intention.

3 The name of each member of the group written on a large label.

4 To prepare each person *the day before* their turn so that they have time to think about what they want to say, or find someone else to speak for them, or ask the group leader to speak for them.

5 Some music for reflection.

There are many ways of using the group register or name list. The following are a few suggestions.

▷ The group is gathered together in a semicircle so that they can all see the focal point.

▷ A group member is then invited to explain to the group how they would like the time together to be used. (This could be a special intention, which can be personal or general. This is then shared with the group.)

▷ Take time to think about the intention and, if appropriate, individual thoughts can be shared with the whole group.

or

▷ A group member may wish everyone to think about a world issue. A short presentation may be prepared and given to inform the group. Time is then taken for reflection and/or prayer.

or

▷In the case where it is difficult to get someone to speak in public then they can enlist the help of any other member(s) of the group to assist them.

or

▷It can often be very effective simply to place the person's name on a special notice-board in the room or at a focal point and allow a quiet time, accompanied by music, for everyone to think about or pray for that person, their family and their situation.

▶3
Using flowers

YOU WILL NEED:

1 A flower for each member of the group (don't forget to include yourself). Collect flowers from the garden or ask people to bring them. There is no need to spend a lot of money.

2 A container or flower vase, with water in it, in a central position in the centre of the room.

3 Six small candles or votive lights. (These can be easily obtained from your nearest church.)

4 To arrange the chairs in a semicircle around the flower container.

5 To select some quiet reflective music.

▷ As the group assembles allow people time to settle and put down everything that they might be holding in their hands or carrying on their back.

▷ Explain that they will have everything they need for this session given to them.

▷ Place the candles around the vase.

▷ Show them the empty vase and a flower. Invite the group to think quietly about the times when they might be given one flower, e.g. at a wedding as a buttonhole, as a sign of affection (a single red rose), a flower laid on the coffin of someone they love, or if the giver just can't afford any more!

▷ Explain that everyone is to be invited to come forward one at a time, pick up a flower and place it in the vase. As they do so they are to think of someone very special to them. It may be that this person is in some kind of need or they may have much to say thank you for to this person. This can either be done silently, or if anyone wishes, they can say the name of the person that their flower is for. Remember to stress that everyone is free to do this silently if they would prefer.

▷ Before the first person comes forward, play your music as a background. It might be necessary to call each person in turn to keep order and allow the symbolism to really speak to the group.

▷ Don't rush, allow a short time for reflection between the placing of each flower.

▷ Conclude with a short reading from scripture, a poem or prose, if you wish, e.g. an adapted version of Matthew 7:7–10:

Jesus said, 'Ask and it will be given to you; search, and you will find; knock, and the door will be opened to you. For if you ask you will receive, if you search you will find, if you knock the door will always be opened to you.'

▶4
Using a mirror

YOU WILL NEED:

1 A small mirror for each person.

2 Paper and pencils for writing.

3 A collection of photographs of one member of the group at different ages.

4 A candle.

5 A small table, decorated to be used as the focal point.

6 To arrange the seating in a semicircle around the table.

7 Some reflective music.

▷ Once the group has settled, invite the person who has brought the photographs to show them to the group.

▷ Notice the different reactions to the photographs: the younger the child in the picture, the greater the compliments!

▷ For the latest 'picture' look at the person.

▷ Ask what the 'picture' captures of the real person. Talk about this.

▷ Invite each person to find a partner. One takes a pencil and paper and the other a mirror, *face down* to begin with. Now explain that the person who has the paper has to write down everything that the other person says about themselves when they look in the mirror. (They are free to say whatever they like.)

▷ They have one minute to do this. Now change over so the other person has the mirror for a minute and their partner becomes the writer. It will be necessary for the group leader to supervise the time on each occasion.

▷ Come back into the group and ask each partner to share what the *other* person said about themselves.

▷When the group has calmed down, discuss whether the comments were mostly negative or positive. What does this tell us about how we see ourselves?

▷To conclude, play some quiet music and ask the group members to reflect on the good things about themselves.

▷If appropriate, invite each person to share with the group something about themselves for which they would like to thank God.

▶5
Using portraits

YOU WILL NEED:

1 To arrange the chairs in a circle.

2 A piece of paper on each chair.

3 A pen or pencil for each member of the group.

4 Some suitable quiet music whilst people move round the circle.

▷Invite each person to sit down and hold a piece of paper.

▷Explain to the group that it is very seldom that we really listen to the good things said about ourselves by other people.

▷Today group members are being invited to write down something good that they would really like to say to each person in the group. Stress that these are comments to build up and help the person to see the good gifts that they have and the gift that they are in themselves.

▷Each member of the group is then invited to put their own name at the top of the page and to place the paper on their chair.

▷They are then free to go *silently* to any chair in the room and write their comments.

▷Play the quiet music to aid concentration as the group moves round.

▷When everyone has finished writing on all the papers, they return silently to their own chairs, and read their 'portraits'.

▷As members of the group are reading their portraits, light the candle and suggest that each person thinks silently about what has been written.

▷All spend a few minutes trying to understand the mystery of *who they are* as individuals and the many gifts that they have been given, some of which they still have to discover.

▶6
Using photographs

YOU WILL NEED:

1 To ask each member of the group to bring a photograph of themselves taken with some friends or their family. If they wish, they can also bring in their photograph albums.

2 A table with a candle.

3 A photograph album arranged on the table with the candle.

4 To arrange the seating in a circle around the table.

5 To select a song/hymn about being with friends and people you love.

6 Paper and pen for each member of the group.

▷Gather the group around the table.

▷Explain that the group is going to look at photographs of happy moments and people that individual members care about.

▷Invite each member of the group to talk about one of their photographs and why it has been chosen from all the others.

▷ Play the music quietly in the background and spend a few minutes thinking of the people that the group have been talking about.

▷ Take the candle from the table and hand it to one of the group who is then asked to say the names of the people in their photograph as they hold the candle.

▷ Pause for a moment for the group to think and/or pray for them.

▷ When everyone has spoken and named particular friends, return the candle to the table.

OFFERING

7
Using incense

YOU WILL NEED:

1 Some grains of incense, a piece of charcoal and a thurible of some kind. For this, you can use any fireproof container, like an earthenware bowl, metal container, etc. Your local priest or school chaplain should be able to help you.

2 Some sand or dry earth to fill your thurible to just below the rim so that everyone can see the charcoal and incense burning. This will also serve to put the charcoal out when necessary.

3 A small table or stool to place the thurible on so that everyone can see.

4 To arrange the seating in a semicircle around the focal point.

5 Matches and taper to light the charcoal.

▷Settle the group around the thurible. Explain that today they will be using incense. Give each member of the group a grain of incense. Ask everyone to look at the incense carefully as it sits in the palm of their hand.

▷Explain that incense comes from the sap of a tree. Fragrances are added so that when the incense is burnt the smoke carries the scent with it and fills the atmosphere.

▷Show the group the piece of charcoal. Note that it is black and dead; it does nothing as it is, except make a mess. It could be used to draw with but even then it remains something very dead.

▷Now explain that you are going to light the charcoal with a flame and ask them to watch very carefully what happens to the charcoal.

▷Light the charcoal from a taper. It is a good idea not to use a match as this will not burn long enough for the charcoal to ignite. This would spoil the effect and atmosphere you have created and burn your fingers!

▷ Gently blow on the edge of the charcoal as it starts to change colour. You will notice it turns grey first before going red. Point out to the group that your breath is blowing life into the charcoal.

▷ Place the charcoal on the sand or dry earth in the thurible.

▷ Take a few grains of incense and place them on the burning charcoal.

▷ Explain the symbolic 'rising up' of the smoke and how this is often used in religious rites to symbolize the 'making holy', 'offering' and 'giving to God' of a person, place, object, or prayer.

▷ Invite each member of your group to come forward, one at a time, and place their grain of incense on the charcoal. As the amount of incense increases so too will the smoke. Be ready for this.

▷ Allow the group time to question and discuss what you have shared with them. Parallels may be drawn between this gesture of burning incense and the Holy Spirit, the breath of God, the giving of life, the kiss of life.

▷ If appropriate, invite the group to think of someone or something they wish to bring before God as the incense rises up.

This idea can be adapted as a penitential service or prayer, the grain of incense being used to symbolize something that members of the group wish to ask forgiveness for or a hurt received that they wish to be healed.

This celebration might conclude with a suitable piece of music or song.

▶8
Using gifts

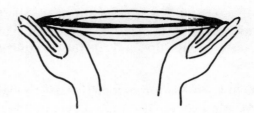

YOU WILL NEED:

1 A paten or plate.

2 A small table.

3 To arrange the seating around the table so that everyone can see easily.

4 To select a song/hymn or piece of music on the theme of giving and offering.

5 A small piece of paper and pen, for each person to write one or two sentences.

▷ Settle the group around the table with the paten/plate in the centre of the table.

▷ Explain that the group is invited to think about their gifts. (Not just their ability to do things, but the gift that they are to other people.)

▷ Spend a few minutes thinking about the ways in which we are a 'gift' to one another, e.g. friendship, helpfulness, kindness, acceptance, loyalty.

▷ In pairs, talk about the gifts that are most valued in themselves and in a friend.

▷ Give each member of the group a piece of paper and pen.
Write down:
(a) One gift for which you would like to thank God.
(b) One gift which you will make a special effort to offer someone today.

▷ As the group members write their thoughts down, play the song/music as a background.

▷ Explain that in a few minutes each person is going to be invited to place their 'offering' on the plate/paten. This symbolizes a desire to offer something of themselves for other people.

▷Having written down their offerings, one member of the group at a time places their paper on the paten/plate. This can be done as the plate is passed round, or the group can go to the table one at a time.

▷Conclude with a few minutes' silent thought about the ways that these offerings really can be put into practice today.

9
Using fire

YOU WILL NEED:

1 To arrange the seating so that the group has a clear view of the focal point.

2 An urn, earthenware vase, or metal container.

3 To half fill the container with sand.

4 A candle.

5 A small piece of paper and pen for each member of the group.

6 Appropriate hymns and music on the theme of forgiveness.

▷Gather the group around your fireproof container. Talk about the power of *fire* with the group. Stress the positive attributes of fire. It strengthens. It purifies, gives warmth and light.

▷Light the candle and place it next to the urn.

▷Either read or talk about the story of the Prodigal Son or some other story (e.g. the woman caught in adultery) that illustrates God's great desire to forgive.

▷Allow a few moments for reflection. Talk about each of the characters in the story. Try to see the point of view of each one. How would they have felt? Why do the group think that they behaved in the way that they did? Who was hurt the most? Who had the most to forgive? Were they really forgiven?

▷Ask each person to write down on a piece of paper something that they would like to ask forgiveness for. Stress that this is completely confidential and no one else is going to see it.

▷Either sing or listen to the selected music while the person leading the reflection time lights their piece of paper from the candle and places it in the urn.

▷Each member of the group is then invited to do likewise.

▷Allow the group time to watch the papers burning. Explain that just as fire purifies gold, so too, through the symbolic action of placing into the fire the area in their lives in need of forgiveness, they are symbolically asking for purification, strength and light.

▷Explain that by the time we have turned and asked for forgiveness from God . . . God has already set out to meet us. (Prodigal Son)

▷Conclude by offering each other the sign of peace.

▶ 10
Using dead leaves

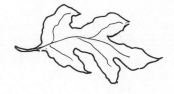

YOU WILL NEED:

1 A small table, a cloth to cover the table, candles, a crucifix, a Bible, a collection of dead leaves.

2 To choose a few slides of trees at different times of the year to illustrate your guided reflection. If this is not possible due to lack of equipment, pictures or posters of trees and leaves at different times of the year can be just as effective.

3 To arrange the room so that everyone can see the special table or altar.

4 To ask for volunteers who might like to help you get the room ready, and to prepare for the time together.

5 To select a suitable piece of music or song.

—As part of the celebration you may wish to ask group members to illustrate their thoughts in some artistic way in their journals.

—This idea could last for more than one session, so don't rush. Allow all the time necessary and if the group would like to develop the idea further then this could be worked out for the next session.

▷ Gather the group around a table that has been specially prepared for the celebration.

▷ If you are going to use slides to illustrate your reflections have people ready to turn out lights, if necessary, before the celebration begins.

▷ One member of the group places an open Bible near the table. Another places a lighted candle near the Bible.

▷ The dead leaves are then laid out on the floor. Allow the group time to think about them. Once they were hidden within branches, then they were buds, and with the spring rains and the warmth of the sun, they broke into fresh green leaves. . . .

▷ Pause for reflection.

▷ For a few months the leaves grew, fed the tree, gave shelter and even food for some animals and insects. In time, their task was complete. With the autumn, they changed colour, began to dry up and eventually fell to the ground. . . .

▷ Pause for reflection.

▷ This might appear to be the end of their life . . . but they still continue. The coloured leaves provide a beautiful carpet of oranges, reds, yellows, browns. They give pleasure to us as we walk through them. Slowly, they begin to break up and form a compost which, in turn, nourishes the ground and gives life back to the tree for the next year – not only to the tree but to all the other flowers and plants where the leaves have fallen.

▷ Pause for reflection.

▷Explain that today members of the group are invited to think of someone they want to remember who has died.

▷The leaf is going to be a symbol of that person.

▷Each member of the group is then invited to pick up a leaf and move to the Bible, touch the Bible with the leaf and then place the leaf on the table, naming the person who has died as they do so.

▷As each person moves in turn to place their leaf on the table, play a suitable piece of music or sing a song/hymn that fits the occasion.

▷Conclude with a suitable reading or prayer, e.g. John 14:1–3.

> Do not let your hearts be troubled.
> Trust in God still, and trust in me.
> There are many rooms in my Father's house;
> If there were not I should have told you.
> I am going now to prepare a place for you
> and after I have gone and prepared you a place,
> I shall return to take you with me;
> So that where I am
> you may be too.

THE WORD

▶11
Using a reading or hymn

YOU WILL NEED TO:

1 Find a reading (not too long) that means something to your group. This does not necessarily have to be religious but something which will make the group think.

or

Select a hymn that will speak to the group. Remember that this does not have to be sung.

2 Select a suitable extract of quiet music to accompany the spoken word and to provide a background in the quiet moments for thoughts and prayer.

Prepare the reading beforehand. An individual or group should always practise, thereby avoiding the embarrassment of not doing themselves justice.

Have a copy of your reading or hymn for each member of the group.

▷ Having arranged the room and the focal point, play the accompanying piece of music as the group settles down.

▷ Give each person a copy of the extract that you have chosen. A reader or a group of readers present the short reading in a suitable manner.

▷ Allow time for the group silently to re-read the passage and think about it. The background music which you have pre-selected will help to dispel any self-consciousness.

▷ After a few minutes, invite those who wish to repeat a phrase or line of the text that has meant something to them. Stress that it does not matter if someone has already said 'their' bit.

▷ When a few minutes have passed after the last speaker, re-read the whole extract to finish off.

▷ Do not hurry the reflection. One passage well used is better than many passages that wash over the heads of the group because they have not had time to take them in.

▶12-16
Using the Word

YOU WILL NEED TO:

1 Find the scripture readings for the day using a daily missal.

2 Prepare a Table of the Word. This can be done either by using a small table with a book stand or cushion to hold the Word or by using a lectionary, if you have one.

3 Place the table in a position so that everyone can see it clearly.

(This idea is one that can last for a day or be the main framework for reflection over a long period.)

4 Prepare the extract with the reader the day before. It is sometimes very difficult to read out a passage of scripture well unless the reading has been practised and understood beforehand.

A note on translations
Using scripture for prayer/reflection must be done in a way that is suitable for your group. The translation and size of print will make a big difference. The Good News Bible, the Revised Standard Version or the Jerusalem Bible are the more suitable translations for most students. The Good News version is best used with a younger age group.

▶12

Using the 'Word' for the day

▷Settle the group around the Table of the Word. Explain that during the celebration of the Eucharist there are two tables: the Table of the Word and the Table of Sacrifice.

▷Invite someone to read a passage. This can be from any of the readings for the day.

▷With a friend, share thoughts on the passage.

▷Ask the question, 'What do we think this is saying to us in our situation today?'

▷Gather up the thoughts of the group and spend a few moments silently thinking about them.

▷If the group members are using journals then they can write down the scripture reference and what they felt it said to them.

▷This process can be repeated each day with different readings. Sometimes they can be acted out rather than read, or presented through drawings and music.

▶13

Using words – telling stories from scripture

The scriptures are full of stories, both the Old Testament and the New. Many young people enjoy acting. Allow the group to look at the stories from the New Testament. Many of these parables are very familiar to them. Spend some time selecting the ones that they feel really say something relevant to them. Invite them to enter imaginatively into the story: identifying with one of the characters, imagining all aspects of their life – the atmosphere, the clothes, the sights and smells – and their hopes and fears.

or

Divide into small groups to act out a modern-day equivalent. Once you have divided everyone into small groups, one for each of the characters involved, ask each small group to think about the character they represent, then invite one person from each group to act out the story from the point of view of that character. Invite group members to think about their feelings towards each character and to share their thoughts, if they so wish.

You may well find that you have at least a week's material before you. Set up a timetable so that each group knows when it is their turn. This will help to keep order each day and set deadlines against groups saying 'we're not ready'.

After the presentation of each story invite the group to spend time thinking about what they have seen and heard. Invite people to enter their thoughts into their journals if they wish.

Scripture commentaries should be available in your school library and in the RE department. In the case of a parish group, your parish priest will certainly have them. If you are not sure of a passage and a group wants help, these commentaries will provide all you need. Older groups will be able to do this research on their own.

It is important to help the group to understand that the Word speaks to us all in different ways and at different times. What might mean a lot to you one day might just float off you the next. Explain that the scripture is very deep. We need to keep going back to it day after day to fathom its meaning.

▶14
Using words – the creative power of words

▷ Gather the group around the Table of the Word.

▷ Give each member of the group a piece of paper and something to write with. Journals could also be used here.

▷ Talk about the *power of words* with the group. Show how words can be used to build people up, make them feel better. Just as words can be also used to destroy and pull them down.

▷ Ask each person to write down the words that they most enjoy hearing or the ones they like to say the most.

▷ Now ask each person to say if they hear those words said to them very often. (They do not have to reveal what the words are unless they wish.)

▷ Having shared this with the group, now think of the people who live with you at home. Choose one person. What do you think they would like to hear from *you*? Write that down. How often do you say these words to them?

▷ Now ask the group to consider how often they use words that hurt or destroy. Why do they do this? This can either be discussed, written down, or both, if appropriate.

▷ What are the words that hurt them the most? Can they say why?

▷ Open the Word at Genesis 1:1–31. Paraphrase the verses for the group showing that when God spoke life was created. What God created was *good*, e.g. 'God said, "Let there be light," and there was light . . . God saw that the light was good . . .'

▷ When God speaks something good is created. What happens when we speak? How is this a challenge for us today?

▷ Share thoughts on this. Perhaps as a conclusion to the reflection time the group could commit themselves to using only *good* words for a day.

▶15
Using the Word to live by

▷Assemble the group around the Table of the Word.

▷Invite someone to read from the book of Deuteronomy 11:18–20:

> Let these words of mine remain in your heart and in your soul: fasten them on your hand as a sign and on your forehead as a circlet. Teach them to your children and say them over to them, whether at rest in your house or walking abroad, at your lying down or at your rising. Write them on the doorposts of your house and on your gates . . .

▷Discuss why this part of the Jewish Law is so detailed about where the Law of God should be written. What do they think is the reason for this?

▷Ask the group members to think about themselves and their homes, as the reading mentions. Select from scripture sayings and short verses that they might like to put in different places in their homes as a reminder of what it is to be a Christian, for example:

> This is what Yahweh asks of you, to act justly, to love tenderly and to walk humbly with your God. (Micah 6:8)

> Into your hands, O Lord, I commend my spirit. (Psalm 31(30):5)

> Grant to us, O Lord, a heart renewed. (Psalm 51(50):10)

> I have carved you on the palm of my hand. (Isaiah 49:16)

> You are precious in my eyes and I love you. (Isaiah 43:4)

> Since God has loved us so much we should love one another. (1 John 4:11)

> Do not be afraid, for I have redeemed you. (Isaiah 43:1)

> I have called you by your name and you are mine. (Isaiah 43:1)

▷There are also all the 'Jesus said' verses, for example:

> I am the Light of the world. (John 8:12)

> I am the Good Shepherd. (John 10:11)

▷The group might like to work in pairs to help find verses.

▷Invite the group members to share their choice of verses and say why they chose them.

▷Spend a few final moments silently reflecting on the implications of living by their verses.

▶16
Using words – one for the day

This idea is also one which can run for some time. The idea is to allow each member of the group to choose *one word* from scripture that means something to them.

▷Gather the group around the Bible. Invite the person whose turn it is to go to the Word and read the sentence that contains their word.

▷Ask them to share with the group why they have chosen the word and a few thoughts on what it means to them in their life today.

▷This is most effective if it is not commented on and the group is allowed to reflect silently on what has been shared. This will also help the reader not to be nervous about someone questioning them or disagreeing.

▷This can be adapted so that more than one person shares a word.

▷Conclude by asking the group to think of ways in which they can live that word for the day. Discuss this together. Those who wish to might enter the word for the day into their journals.

▶17
Using letters

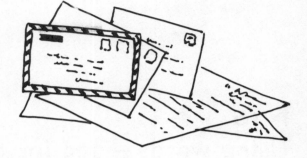

1 Some writing paper and an envelope for each member of the group.

2 A Bible.

3 A candle.

4 Some reflective music.

5 An example of someone separated from the person they love. Their only means of keeping in touch is by letter. For example, the following is a true story of a seven-year-old boy sent from Nigeria to school in England:

The letter

This was the fifth time that I had been to the station that day and not once had the train been on time. The 8 p.m. InterCity was bringing the last of my new boys, a seven-year-old from Nigeria. I knew little about him except a series of calls from the Nigerian High Commission and a rather frosty letter from a gentlemen who would be delivering the child into my care that evening.

Twenty-five minutes late, the train pulled into the station. There, walking towards me, was a very tall man with a very small boy. A porter followed carrying his trunk. 'Miss Castle?' enquired the tall man. 'Yes, Welcome to . . .' and before I could say another word, the little boy was thrust forward. 'This is Chuka. I will collect him from your school on December 10th.' With that he walked back for the next London-bound train.

Too stunned to say anything I reached down and took the little boy's hand. He was shaking with fright. I squeezed his hand gently to try and reassure him, but there was no response.

I had long since learnt not to try and make small talk with little children when they are deeply upset. This one was no exception. I just hoped that the children back at school would soon bring him round.

Having introduced Chuka to some of the lads his age and showed him where his bed was, I thought that in the circumstances I would help him unpack. Eager hands reached out to greet the new boy. No response. 'Take Chuka and show him the games room', I said, hoping that that would help to break the ice. Off he was dragged. I knew that they understood how he would be feeling. Hadn't they too felt that awful pain of being alone and longing just to go home?

Breakfast is always a rowdy affair. Only one thing brings instant silence. The moment the prefect hands the duty teacher the post. Letters from home. All heads turn. Eyes riveted to the pile of mail. Ears pricked for one name only. Theirs.

To ease the moment I always arranged the post in alphabetical order.

I had not expected a letter for Chuka in the first few days, knowing how long it can take for letters from abroad to get here. But all my boys from overseas had now had their first letters, except Chuka. I could not believe that he had been forgotten so quickly. We had been in school two weeks and not a single letter for this lad. The more I thought about the way in which this child had arrived, the more angry I became.

'Russell . . . Songa . . . Sullivan . . . and Williams.' End of the mail. Nothing for Chuka. I looked up and saw his two huge brown eyes fill up with tears yet again.

As Chuka filed out with the rest I put my hand on his shoulder. 'Perhaps tomorrow love . . . they won't have forgotten you', I said hopefully and then wished immediately that I hadn't.

The next morning I quickly sorted through the post looking for one letter. There it was. An African stamp and the letter was addressed to Chuka! I wanted to rush into the dining room and give it to him straight away. But I knew that that kind of treatment was not a good idea.

Silence fell as I called out Chuka's name. I waited for him to come forward. He didn't move. So I repeated his name. Slowly, he came forward and took the letter. I looked into his blank face to see if there was any glimmer of joy. Nothing. He put the letter into his inside pocket and sat down.

Registration always follows breakfast. I was not too surprised to find Chuka missing from class. Leaving one of the sixth form in charge I went to Chuka's room to find him. Sure enough he was there. Tears streaming down his face as he sat staring at his letter. The letter that already he knew by heart. We sat for a few minutes in silence and then I told him that he could stay there until he was ready to join us.

By break time Chuka was back in class and what a different boy. He smiled for the first time. I noticed what a handsome young man he was. Now perhaps he might settle and begin to enjoy life with his new friends.

Lunch time came and went and once again the boys were lined up for class. I was just settling everyone down when the house prefect tore into the room and asked me to come quickly as Chuka was tearing the house apart.

I would never have believed that such roaring and chaos could result from one seven-year-old boy. It took every inch of Leonard's six foot four to catch and contain Chuka.

'Chuka, what on earth is the matter with you?' I roared.

'My letter', he wailed, 'Someone's taken my letter.'

No wonder he was ripping the place apart! 'Chuka, you must not accuse people of taking your things. Where did you leave your letter?' That, I thought, was a pretty stupid question on my part, small boys always leave their letters in the same places, either in their inside pockets to be transferred to under their pillows at night, or under their pillow.

'Under my pillow', he sobbed.

I turned to get Leonard's help to tidy up, but he had already gone. So I told Chuka that I would send some boys over to help him tidy up. Then we would see what we could do to find the letter. But before I was going to leave him he had to calm down and come to the kitchen with me for a cool drink.

As we sat in the kitchen the door opened. There stood Leonard with Antonio, looking very sorry for himself. Antonio walked up to Chuka and handed him his letter. 'I'm sorry Chuka, it was only a joke.'

'Some joke!' said Leonard.

'Well, Antonio, perhaps you could make up for your joke by clearing up this mess', I suggested.

Chuka carefully checked that his letter was intact and put it into his inside jacket pocket and smiled up at Leonard.

Chuka stayed with us for eleven years. He never received another letter from his home. Every holidays he was collected from school by the same austere gentlemen who neither spoke nor smiled.

Chuka and I became great friends. He had grown into a fine young man who was much admired for his strength of character and sense of fun. On the day that he left we were sitting in the kitchen drinking coffee when he suddenly said 'Miss Castle, do you remember the day I nearly wrecked this place?'

'Yes, I certainly do Chuka', I replied with a grin.

'Well Miss, I've still got that letter. Would you like to see it?'

I was stunned. Chuka had never spoken about his home life and I had never questioned him on it. In schools like ours you learn when to keep silent.

'Well, Chuka, that's private and I don't want to pry.'

'No, Miss, I want you to share it with you.' Slowly he took out his letter and handed it to me. It was very faded now and almost transparently thin from so much handling. The letter read:

'My dearest Son,

'We are heartbroken that you had to be taken from us so quickly. But the fighting has already claimed the lives of your mother and brothers. I dare not risk losing you. I arranged for a loyal Government friend to smuggle you out of Nigeria to England. He tells me that now you are safe there and when you are a man you will be able to return to our country. Please God peace will then reign in our hearts and in our land. Remember who you are and what you must do for your people. I cannot write again my son, until there is peace, for fear that your life will be in danger.

'Remember always that your father and your family love you.'

Suddenly, everything fell into place. The stranger who brought Chuka and was soon to collect him. Chuka's distress at losing his letter and the mystery that always surrounded him.

'Thank you, Chuka. Can I ask you just one thing?'

'Yes, Miss Castle.'

'May I write to you?'

Chuka smiled. 'Yes, Miss Castle. I would like that very much.'

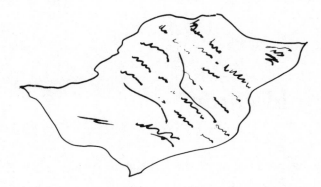

▷ Gather the group around the candle and the Table of the Word.

▷ Give everyone a piece of writing paper and an envelope.

▷ Spend a few minutes talking about letters and what they are. How do you feel when you receive one from someone who is very special to you?

▷ What do you do with the letter when you have finished reading it? If you keep it, where do you put it? Why do you put it in that place?

▷ Do you re-read the letter? How often? Why do you think you do this?

▷ Read or tell the story of Chuka, or a story of your own.

▷ Allow the group a few minutes' silent reflection at the end of the story.

▷ Draw the group's attention to the Bible. Here is another 'letter' from someone who loves us very much. Someone who gave us life as Chuka's father and mother gave him life. Like Chuka, we too are separated from seeing this person. What we have are their words. That is what the Bible is. God's word, God's letter to us. It contains the story of who we are and what we are called to do. In the same way that Chuka's father asks him to remember who he is, what he has to do for his people and never to forget how much he is loved.

▷Imagine that you have one chance to write a letter that can be taken to God. What would you write?

▷Invite the group to write their letters whilst you play some reflective music in the background.

▶18
Using old cards

YOU WILL NEED:

1 To collect old cards of any kind that can be cut up.

2 Scissors and glue.

3 Sugarpaper or light card.

4 A collection of pens and colouring materials.

▷The group will need access to tables for this session.

▷Spend a few minutes talking about why people send cards. Explore as many of the reasons as possible.

▷Ask members of the group how they feel when they receive a card. What does it mean to them? Where do they put it? Do they keep it for a long time?

▷Invite the group members to think of someone special and to make their own card for this person by cutting up the cards you have provided.

▷Ask them to think of why they are going to send it. Encourage the group to think of someone who would really appreciate the thought, especially someone who may not get many cards.

▷Write a special message telling that person that they are cared about and not forgotten.

▷Don't forget to post the card!

▶19–21
Using the O antiphons

YOU WILL NEED:

1 To prepare a short introduction explaining what the O antiphons are, e.g. 'The O antiphons are prayers composed by the early Christian Church. They symbolize the longing by the early Christians for the final coming of the Messiah. They are now used by the Christian Church in its liturgy during the last week before Christmas.'

2 *The O antiphons:*

17th Dec.   'O Wisdom, you come forth from the mouth of the Most High. You fill the universe and hold all things together in a strong yet gentle manner. O come to teach us the way of truth.'

18th Dec.   'O Adonai and leader of Israel, you appeared to Moses in a burning bush and you gave him the Law on Sinai. O come and save us with your mighty power.'

19th Dec.   'O Stock of Jesse, you stand as a signal for the nations; Kings fall silent before you whom the peoples acclaim. O come to deliver us and do not delay.'

20th Dec.   'O Key of David and sceptre of Israel, what you open no one else can close again; what you close no one can open. O come to lead the captive from prison; free those who sit in darkness and the shadow of death.'

21st Dec   'O Rising Sun, you are the splendour of eternal light and the sun of justice. O come and enlighten those who sit in darkness and in the shadow of death.'

22nd Dec.   'O king whom all peoples desire, you are the corner stone which makes all one. O come and save us whom you made from clay.'

23rd Dec.   'O Immanuel, you are the king and judge, the One whom the peoples await and their Saviour. O come and save us, Lord, our God.'

(Taken from *Morning and Evening Prayer*, Collins.)

Another translation of the O antiphons can be found in the familiar form of the carol 'O come, O come, Emmanuel'.

3 Copies of the O antiphons for the group and the carol 'O come, O come, Emmanuel' for each member of the group to work with.

4 Paper, colours, paints, etc., for illustrations. You may wish to use the group's work for decorating the room or church.

▶19
Using the O antiphons – making modern versions

▷Give each member of the group a copy of the carol 'O come, O come, Emmanuel'. Sing or recite the carol.

▷Having sung the carol through once, ask the group to work with a partner and see if they could re-write one verse of the carol in a modern language version and setting, or write what they think the verse could mean if it was to be written today.

▷Some group members might find it easier to express their thoughts and interpretation through art work.

▷Invite each pair to share their thoughts with the group.

▶20
Symbolizing the O antiphons

"O RISING SUN"

▷Give each member of the group a copy of the O antiphons.

▷Read them together, one at a time.

▷After the reading of each antiphon, talk about what the group thinks it meant when it was written, and what it might mean for them today.

▷Talk about what symbol might be used for each of the antiphons.

▷ Using journals or pieces of paper invite each member of the group to draw/paint a symbol for each of the antiphons.

▷ Ask the group members to work in silence and think about what they are working on.

▷ It might be helpful to play a version of the carol from a tape or record as a background to their quiet time.

▷ If the group wishes, display their symbols in the room or church.

▶21
Using the O antiphons – making your own acclamation

▷ Open the reflection/prayer time by singing the carol 'O come, O come, Emmanuel'.

▷ Give each member of the group a copy of the O antiphons.

▷ Talk about them and ask the group to say what they think they could mean for us today.

▷ Ask the group to think of words which in some way depict God for them, e.g. *bread, rainbow, light, hope, fire, shepherd, star, wisdom, peace, love, water, king.*

▷ As the group members suggest words, ask one member to make a list of them on the board or on a large piece of paper for all to see.

▷ Invite each person to select one word and compose an acclamation.

▷ Suggest that the group works silently.

▷ Play some peaceful music in the background to aid concentration and reflection.

▷ When the group has finished, invite those who wish to share their acclamations with the group to do so. Allow a few moments' silent reflection after each acclamation.

SYMBOLS

22

Using images and symbols

YOU WILL NEED:

1 A collection of religious symbols and objects that may remind the group of God. Choose a good variety but not too many, e.g. Pictures. These can be religious ones or pictures that are inspirational in some way.

Crosses, there are many different kinds

A candle	A father
A flower	A mother
A icon	A cloud
A bulb, breaking into flower	The sky
A baby or child	Water/the sea
A lamb	Fire
The sun	Beautiful landscape

2 To invite a group of helpers to prepare the room before the group begins this session.

3 To arrange your symbols so that each one can be clearly seen by the whole group.

4 To make sure that the room is arranged in such a way that the group can write down their thoughts during the session without too much movement or disturbance.

5 To select some quiet music that will help to keep the atmosphere calm and recollected whilst the group is writing.

▷ Having settled the group and seen that everyone has their journal or a piece of paper to write on, spend a few minutes talking about each of the symbols.

▷Ask the group members to say what the symbols mean to them.

▷In pairs discuss which of the symbols are liked the best and which are liked the least.

▷Ask the members of the group if there are any symbols that they can think of that symbolize God for them. *Discuss these.*

▷Invite each person to write in their journal (if appropriate), or on a piece of paper, which of the symbols speaks most to them and why.

▷If anyone feels that none of the selected symbols are helpful because they don't believe in God, then ask them to select one that best symbolizes what they have learnt about Christianity, and say why.

▷It might be helpful to the group if some reflective music was played during the writing period.

▶23
Using candles

YOU WILL NEED TO:

1 Arrange the room so that the group can sit in a circle.

2 Place a large candle in the centre of the circle. If you are not able to find a large candle, then use the largest that you can find, but place it on a stand or table for all to see clearly.

3 Collect together enough smaller candles so that each member of the group will be able to have one. (It might be helpful to prepare wax shields to fit on to the candle to prevent wax dripping onto clothes or carpets! These can be easily made by using circles of stiff paper or light cardboard. See diagram opposite.)

4 Select a piece of music, or a song, that fits the theme of light.

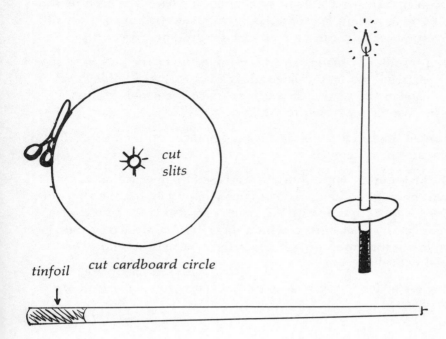

tinfoil cut cardboard circle

cut slits

▷ Settle the group as they come into the room. If it is possible, darken the room so that the effect of the candlelight is shown at its best. The main light of the room should be the central candle. This will help to focus everyone's attention as the time begins.

▷ Explain that the only light in the room is going to be candlelight.

▷ Ask the group if they can think of a way in which the light of the one candle can be increased . . . without touching the candle or setting the place on fire!

▷ Invite each member of the group to come forward and receive a candle and light it from the main candle. Having lit their candle they then return to their place.

▷ Play some quiet music as each person comes forward and lights their candle.

▷ Talk about the increase in warmth and the effect of so many candles now being alight.

▷ What does candlelight do? How does it feel? What kind of atmosphere is created?

▷Explain that the central light symbolizes the love that each person has burning within. It can be kept for ourselves, but then it will do very little, or it can be used to light up other lives.

▷Ask a member of the group to say the name of the person sitting on their right. As they call out the name, they gently blow out their candle. (Be careful of wet wax. Hold the candle still until the hot wax is set.)

▷When all the candles are out, again comment on the loss of light. Compare the difference.

▷Ask the group to write down/or discuss in pairs/groups, a time when through the kindness of someone else they felt the effect of being loved. If appropriate the group can also talk about a time when the love that burned within them was dampened or put out. Invite the group to talk about their feelings and how they coped with them.

▷Members of the group with a journal can write or illustrate their thoughts.

▶24
Using candles –
'Receive the Light of the World'

YOU WILL NEED TO:

1 Arrange the seating in a circle.

2 Select a suitable piece of music on the theme of *light*.

3 Place a stool or a small table in the centre of the circle.

4 Select a candle that can be handed around the group.

▷In this session the group is invited to sit in a circle around a lighted candle.

▷Explain to the group that after a song/hymn, or piece of music, the lighted candle is going to be passed from one person to the next.

▷ As each person receives the candle they pause for a moment and then say the name of the person next to them, saying '. . . receive the Light of the World'. This person then takes the candle and holds it for a moment. The group then prays for that person silently.

▷ When the candle has completed the circle, it is passed around a second time and each person, as they receive the candle, asks the group to pray for someone for whom they would like a prayer said. (If someone does not wish to ask for prayers, then they simply ask that this person be remembered.)

▷ When the candle has completed the circle for the second time, the group remains silent for a few minutes before the candle is extinguished.

▶25
Using candles

YOU WILL NEED TO:

1 Arrange the seating in a circle as for Preparation 24.

2 Draw the outline of a candle on a sheet of A4 paper. Photocopy this for each member of the group.

3 Select a song or piece of music that relates to the subject of caring for other people, loving them when they are down, and so on.

4 Choose some quiet music to play in the background.

▷ Settle the group in a circle around the central candle.

▷ Give each member of the group their paper candle.

▷As the music plays quietly in the background, ask each member of the group to think of a person that they love, or know about, someone they work with or live with, who they feel is going through a 'dark' time in their lives. Maybe they are depressed, out of work, finding it difficult to cope, for one reason or another.

▷Invite each person to think about what that person really needs to lift the darkness from their life . . . What do they need to hear, come to know, or experience?

▷Write down on the 'candle' what you would wish for them. This can be in the form of a prayer, a poem, or just your wish for them.

▷Conclude by reading together John 8:12: 'Jesus . . . the Light of the World'.

▶26
Using candles – to remember prisoners of conscience

YOU WILL NEED TO:

1 Write to Amnesty International for their education pack and materials on prisoners of conscience:

  Amnesty International, British Section,
  5 Roberts Place,
  London EC1 0EJ.

2 Invite a few of the group to prepare this session with you by selecting the prisoner that they would like to concentrate on. Perhaps they would like to lead the time together?

3 Prepare an *Amnesty candle*, symbol of Amnesty International.

4 Place the candle in the middle of the circle.

5 Select a piece of music on the theme of *freedom*.

▷ This idea could easily develop into something which could last for several days. If the group wishes to go into this area more deeply, invite different members of the group to do research and preparation so that it is not always the same people who are involved.

▷ Settle the group around the Amnesty candle.

▷ Explain what a prisoner of conscience is.

▷ The group may well have prepared some form of display. Make sure that this can be easily seen.

▷ Talk about the symbolism of the candle. The light burning brightly in spite of the barbed wire which symbolizes captivity.

▷ Focus on one prisoner of conscience. Tell their story. Try to understand what it is like not to be free, e.g. construct a small cell in the classroom. Sit someone in it. How long would it be before they got 'fed up'? (This can be easily done by chalking out a small area on the floor and not letting the person move out of the area.) How many steps can they take in any direction? Can they lie down? Stand up?

▷ How would they feel in this situation? Invite the group to share their thoughts and then to think about the prisoner they have chosen in silence for a few moments.

▷ Write a letter to them or make them a card. You may well be able to post these to the prisoner. Amnesty will tell you the address.

▷ Display this prisoner's name and story where it can be easily seen by as many people as possible.

▷ Perhaps you can organize a minute's silence for that person each day for a week. Light the candle when it is 'time to remember'.

▶27
Using candles – lightening the load

YOU WILL NEED TO:

1 Arrange the seating in a circle around a central candle that can be passed around the group.

2 Select a piece of music to go with the idea of caring for one another.

3 Give each member of the group a copy of 'Footprints'.

Footprints

One night a man had a dream. He dreamed he was walking along the beach with the Lord. Across the sky flashed scenes from his life. Each scene, he noticed two sets of footprints in the sand; one belonging to him, and the other to the Lord.

When the last scene of his life flashed before him, he looked back at the footprints in the sand. He noticed that many times along the path of his life there was only one set of footprints. He also noticed that they happened at the very lowest and saddest times of his life.

This really bothered him and he questioned the Lord about it.

'Lord, you said that once I decided to follow you, you'd walk with me all the way. But I have noticed that during the most troublesome times in my life, there is only one set of footprints. I don't understand why when I needed you most you would leave me.'

The Lord replied, 'My precious, precious child, I love you and I would never leave you. During your times of trial and suffering, when you see only one set of footprints,

It was then that I carried you.'

▷ As the group assembles around the candle, give each member a copy of 'Footprints'.

▷ Play your music quietly as each person reads the story for themselves first.

▷ As one of the group to read the story aloud to the whole group.

▷Invite the group to write down on the back of their 'Footprints' either a time that they have helped someone to 'carry their load' or a time when someone has done that for them.

▷Write down how they felt at that time. How did they feel towards the person who had helped them, or they had helped?

▷If the group feels able to do so, invite some people to talk about their experiences.

▶28
Using rings

YOU WILL NEED:

1 To invite a small group to help you gather together different kinds of rings.

2 To arrange the seating around the focal point. Display the rings so that everyone can see them.

3 A candle.

4 To write out the lines of the marriage service which speaks about the rings. ('With this ring, I thee wed.')

▷As the group assembles, light the candle.

▷Ask the preparation group to show the rest of the group the rings that they have collected. Try to say something about each of the rings. When it would be worn, by whom and what it symbolizes.

▷Invite members of the group who may be wearing a ring to tell the group about it. Who gave it to them, or how they got it, etc.

▷Talk about why rings are so special. (They are signs of friendship, love, remembrance.)

▷ Think about a ring that you have been given or one that you gave to someone else. (If this is not applicable, then do this as an imaginative exercise.)

▷ What does the ring mean to you? Is it in memory of something special?

▷ Invite the group to write about this, or to share their thoughts with a partner.

▷ Gather round the candle again and invite members of the group to pray for special people in their lives. People who have given them a ring, or who wear their ring, or someone to whom they would like to give a ring!

▶29
Using a cross

YOU WILL NEED:

1 With a group of helpers, to gather together as many different examples of crucifixes and crosses as you can.

2 To collect short twigs and pieces of string for the group members to make their own crosses.

3 Paper and pencils for each member of the group.

4 To select suitable songs, hymns and poems on the theme of the cross.

5 Pictures from artists on their interpretation of the crucifixion.

6 To prepare a small table with a single cross and a lighted candle.

▷ Gather the group around the table and the cross.

▷ Ask the group to look at the different examples of crosses on their hand-out.

▷ Talk about what a cross is and what it symbolizes.

▷ Get group members to discuss each of the drawings in pairs.

▷ Ask members of the group what they think about the way people are wearing or displaying a cross.

▷ Gather the group together and allow time for each person to say how they feel about the use of crosses.

▷ Give each member of the group two twigs and a piece of string. Make the point that the cross the Jesus died on was not like the jewelled fashionable ones they have been looking at. Rather it was simply two pieces of wood tied or nailed crudely together as part of a bigger structure, a bit like scaffolding. There was nothing beautiful about it at all.

▷ Play music quietly, as the group are invited to make a cross out of their two pieces of wood.

▷ Conclude by reading a short passage from the passion of Jesus, or a suitable poem.

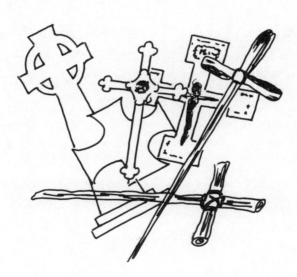

▶30–32
Using water

1 A bowl or an attractive container for water.

2 A candle.

3 A selection of passages on water and blessing from scripture, displayed for all to see, e.g. Psalm 34, Psalm 67, Psalm 128, Psalm 134, Deuteronomy 7:7–14, Deuteronomy 11:26–29, Ephesians 1:3. (These are just a few, there are many more which can be easily traced through a Bible Concordance.)

Possible readings on the theme of water: Psalm 42, 'As a deer longs for running streams'; John 7:37–38, John 4:1–26, Revelation 22:17.

4 Paper and pen for each person.

5 Flowers and greenery to decorate the focal point for the water.

6 A table or stool on which to stand the bowl of water.

7 To invite a few from the group to arrange the table, bowl of water, flowers and candle.

8 To select music/hymns/songs on the theme of water.

9 Slides of water, barren ground with no life, plants in the rain, drops of water on a pool, someone drinking water, etc. can be used as part of the reflection time.

(There are many creative ways of using water for reflection and prayer. The following are just a few to get the group started.)

▶30
Using water – to renew

▷Gather the group around the water.

▷Talk about the different uses of water. Ask the group to say how water feels when you drink it, wash with it, or swim in it.

▷Select one of the readings on the theme of water. Play some quiet music as someone reads the extract. You can also accompany the reading with a few slides.

▷After the presentation of the music, reading and slides invite the group silently to reflect on what they have seen, and think about an area, firstly in their own life, and then in society, that needs to be renewed.

▷If the group wishes they may share some of their thoughts about the way in which they could help to renew the community in which they live.

▶31
Using water – to bless

(This idea is one that could last for several sessions.)

▷Gather the group around the water.

▷Ask for a volunteer to come forward and place their hand in the water and then bless themselves with the water by making the sign of the cross.

▷Talk about what has just happened. What does it mean to the group to bless either yourself, another person or an object?

▷People often say 'God bless you'. What are they saying? What are they expecting to happen?

▷In pairs, think of all the times that people ask for a blessing, e.g. at weddings, at a meal, when they move into a new house, for a new baby, for someone who is sick . . . Gather up the ideas of the group and make a list of them for everyone to see.

▷ Ask the group to work in pairs and choose a few of the ideas and prepare their own blessing ceremony for each idea.

▷ Stress that they do not necessarily need a lot of words. Actions and symbols can also speak.

▷ The 'blessings' can then be gathered up and displayed in a special book to be used by the group at an appropriate time.

▷ When the final part of the session draws to a close, conclude with a simple blessing of the water and one another, e.g. gather the group around the water and display the group's blessings. Light a candle and place it by the bowl of water. Read one of the scripture passages and reflect for a few minutes. Select two members of the group and invite one to hold the bowl and the other to bless each person in turn. Get them to move round the whole group by signing people on the forehead with the blessed water:

> 'Pat, may the Lord bless you';
> 'Joan, I bless you with this water and the love of Jesus Christ';

or any other blessing of their own.

▷ A variation of this could be to allow each person in the group to bless the person next to them.

▶ 32
Using water – to cleanse

▷ Gather the group around the water.

▷ Play some suitable music on the theme of water.

▷ Read the account of Jesus washing the feet of Peter. (John 13:3–11)

▷ Spend a few moments thinking about this passage.

▷ Invite the group to share their ideas about why Jesus washed the feet of the disciples.

▷What did Jesus mean when he said 'If I do not wash you, you can have nothing in common with me'?

▷Talk about the aspects of service for one another and forgiveness that the passage is talking about.

▷As the thoughts of the group are gathered up, invite each group member to place their hands into the water as a symbolic washing. As they do this each person thinks of an area of their life that needs cleansing.

▷A variation on this would be for two people to move round the group, one holding the bowl of water and towel, and the other washing the hands of each person.

▶33
Using oil – as a sign of being chosen

YOU WILL NEED:

1 To decide what kind of celebration this anointing is going to be. An anointing before being sent out to do something special, an anointing as a sign of having been chosen, or an anointing as a sign of love and gladness.

2 Some scented oil in a small dish.

3 A ball of cotton wool to wipe the anointer's fingers.

4 To arrange the focal point so that the container of oil can be seen by the group.

5 Some candles.

6 Some suitable music to fit the aspect of anointing that you have chosen.

7 A copy of Isaiah 43:1–4 for each member of the group or a copy of *Songs of the Spirit* no. 38, 'Do not be afraid'.

8 A small group of people to arrange the focal point.

▷Gather the group around the focal point.

▷Spend a few minutes talking about sacred oil and why it is used, e.g. at baptism, confirmation, holy orders, sacrament of the sick, anointing of kings and queens. Priests, prophets and kings were always seen as God's anointed servants.

▷Talk about how Jesus continues to call people by name to do something special. Every one of us is challenged to take up a role that we alone can fulfil. If we don't accept this, no one else can replace us or contribute what we have to contribute.

▷Sing or recite the song, 'Do not be afraid', *Songs of the Spirit* no. 38, verses 1–5.

or

Read Isaiah 43:1–4.

▷Ask the group members to take one verse at a time and share with a partner what it means for them.

▷Using the words of the song as a prayer of anointing, e.g.

'Steve . . . "I have called you by your name; you are mine" . . . go and spread the good news of the Gospel of Jesus Christ.'

or

'Frances . . . "Remember, you are precious in my eyes . . . Do not be afraid" . . . bring the good news to the poor.'

▷Move around the group anointing each person in turn.

▷Try to find a special anointing prayer suited to each member of the group.

IMAGES

▶34
Using pictures

YOU WILL NEED:

1 A candle.

2 A selection of inspirational pictures from magazines, posters or photographs.

3 To invite a small group to help display the pictures and prepare others for people to use for their reflections. Each person will need one. Choose a very varied selection of pictures.

4 Writing paper and pens for each member of the group.

5 Tables or something for the group members to lean on while they work.

▷ Gather the group around the display of pictures with the lighted candle in the middle.

▷ Explain to the group members that in this session they are going to imagine that they are in one of the pictures.

▷ Invite members to choose a picture that they like and could see themselves in.

▷ Ask group members to discuss with a partner why they chose that picture and then to spend some time thinking alone about the picture.

▷ Write down what you think is happening in the picture. What, in your imagination, are you doing in the picture?

▷ Is what is happening in your picture good or bad? Does it give life or take it away? What do you want to happen and why?

▷ Gather the members of the group together after their reflections and invite anyone who wishes to share their stories to do so.

▷ Talk about these together.

▷ Conclude by silently sitting and looking at the display of pictures around the burning candle.

▶35
Using slides

1 A collection of slides on as many different topics as possible, e.g. slides depicting the beauty of creation, showing young people working together, enjoying life, helping others; or collections of slides on more imaginative themes like beauty, joy, suffering, hope, war, peace, life, death.

2 Reflective music/readings, to go with your theme. If you are using a reading, you will need a candle or torch so that the reader can see.

3 The use of a room that can be darkened or has a day screen.

4 It is not necessary always to use a lot of slides. A few well used with the right text or music are far better than dozens of slides that only leave a vague impression.

5 Make sure that your seating arrangements are such that you will not have to get up and move the group to watch the slides once they are settled. This breaks the atmosphere and can spoil the moment for reflection.

6 Depending on the effect that you are trying to create with your slides, always leave them on the screen long enough for the group to really take them in.

▷Gather the group around the focal point.

▷As the room may well be darkened for most of the session, explain to the group what is going to happen so that everyone is at ease in the situation.

▷The reading of a well-known scripture passage set to modern-day slides can often be both effective and meaningful, e.g. the Parables, hymns, songs, poems, psalms.

▷Leave the last slide on the screen at the end of the presentation to allow for a few moments of concentrated reflection.

▷Another way of ending the session is to silently re-show the slides in reverse order. In this way you will enable the group to think again over the theme.

▶36
Using bricks

YOU WILL NEED:

1 A table.

2 A small pile of bricks; one brick will do if they are hard to find.

3 A candle.

4 Some reflective music.

5 A collection of pictures of brick buildings.

6 To arrange the seating in a semicircle so that everyone can see the bricks and the pictures.

▷When the group is seated, pass one of the bricks around and ask each person in turn to say what they think about it. (This will lead to some amusement which is fine, after all, it is only a brick!)

▷Place the brick where all can see it clearly.

▷Ask the members of the group to name as many uses for the brick as they can.

▷Now show the group the pictures of the buildings and compare them with the single brick or disordered pile of bricks before them.

▷For a few minutes talk about what it involves to progress from a pile of bricks to a building similar to one in the pictures.

▷Ask one of the group to stand up and hold the brick.

▷Ask the group to think silently for a few minutes. What did it take to turn bricks into amazing buildings? It took a master builder and many helpers.

▷Now, think: what does it mean when we say to someone 'You're a real brick'? . . . Someone who can be relied on, who will always do their best for you. Someone who will be there when everyone else deserts you.

▷Invite the group members to share their thoughts.

▷Conclude by listening quietly to the music and considering the question 'What am I being built into and by whom?'

▶37
Using shoes

YOU WILL NEED:

1 A table or stool with a candle.

2 An old worn-out pair of shoes.

3 To arrange the seating in a circle so that everyone can see the shoes.

4 Quiet music for reflection.

5 Copies of a modern hymn book. You will need one for each person.

6 Paper and pen for each person.

▷Gather the group around the table on which are the old shoes and a lighted candle.

▷Talk about the shoes for a few minutes. Notice how old they are and how worn.

▷Notice, too, how they have taken on the shape of the foot of the person that wore them. They have been worn by that person so long that now they will fit no other foot.

▷Think about the service that the pair of shoes has given. Where have they walked?

▷To what occasions have they been worn in their 'best days'? If they could speak what could they tell us of the person who wore them?

▷Ask the group members to think quietly on their own and write down who they think would have worn those shoes. What kind of person? How have the shoes been cared for?

▷As the group is writing, give out the hymn books. When they have finished, ask them to look up in the hymn books lines of hymns that mention walking.

▷Copy out any lines that they think are meaningful.

▷Use these extracts and any thoughts from the group about the owner of the shoes as a basis for a concluding shared reflection.

▷Those who have journals could enter their thoughts.

►38-39
Using hands

YOU WILL NEED:

1 A small table for the Bible and a candle.

2 Some songs/music/hymns on the theme of *hands*.

3 A piece of paper (A4 size) and a pencil for each member of the group.

4 A copy of the line from Isaiah 49:15–16, placed where everyone can see it: 'I will never forget you, I have carved you on the palm of my hand'.

5 To display a copy of the picture 'Praying Hands' by Dürer.

6 The story of Dürer's 'Praying Hands'.

The story of Albrecht Dürer's 'Praying Hands'

There were two brothers, Franz and Albrecht, who were very talented and longed for careers as artists. They came from a large family who were very poor and unable to pay for their studies.

One day Albrecht said to Franz: 'Why don't we take turns to study painting, whilst the other earns the money to pay for it. That way we can both become artists.' Franz agreed, but only if Albrecht, the younger of the two, studied first because he was the better artist.

Albrecht studied hard under the great masters while Franz laboured to keep them both. When Albrecht finished his studies he returned home joyfully to tell Franz it was now his turn. But when Franz held out his hands they were gnarled and calloused, the hands of a worker unable even to hold a pencil, useless to an artist. Albrecht was grief-stricken. 'There is only one thing I can do now to repay you. I shall draw a picture that will speak to people's hearts – a picture of these hands of sacrifice and love.'

Four hundred years later the picture of the 'Praying Hands' is known and loved all over the world. Albrecht Dürer became one of Germany's greatest painters, but his brother to whom he owed his success, whose hands are forever famous, is almost forgotten.

►38
Using hands

▷Gather the group around the table.

▷Invite the group to place their hands in their laps with the palms gently turned upwards.

▷Look at both palms carefully. See the lines, the marks, the cuts, scars, callouses from hard work and the patterns of the skin. Gently turn each hand over and do the same.

▷Divide the group into pairs and ask each pair to compare their hands.

▷Assemble the group together and ask members to hold their hands out into the centre of the group. See how different they all are. Each hand has its own story.

▷Think about the ways your hands have been used in the past few hours. Have they been helpful hands or hurtful?

▷Play some quiet music on the theme of hands, or sing an appropriate song.

▷Talk about ways in which hands can reach out to others in need. Invite each member of the group to think of one way in which they can 'Lend a hand' today.

▷Those who are keeping a journal may want to write down their thoughts.

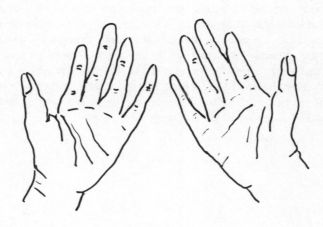

▶39
Using hands – for movement and prayer

(This is a prayer based on an idea by Kevin Yell.)

▷ Gather the group around a lighted candle.

▷ Play some gentle background music.

▷ Ask members of the group to put their hands into their laps.

▷ Ask people to open their fingers and clasp both hands tightly together.

▷ Ask each person to close their eyes and respond to the prayer with their hands.

▷ Talk the group through the following short prayer exercise:

> Jesus, my hands hurt.
> They are so tight.
> Clenched together into a knot.
> My knuckles are white
> Drained of life's blood
> Help me Jesus to let go of all
> that causes me so much tension and hurt.
> Help me to undo my hands
> Jesus as I begin
> to let go
> the blood is coming back into my fingers
> they don't hurt so much
> Now I can see again the marks on my hands
> Finger nails that dug into my flesh
> Help me to let go
> Jesus these hands that have touched so many people
> Forgive the times that they hurt and wounded
> Help them to rest
> open and at peace . . .

▷ Let the music play quietly as the group sits in silence for a few moments.

▶40
Using hands – to pray

▷Invite the group to sit in a semicircle around the Table of the Word.

▷Display the picture of the 'Praying Hands' by Dürer.

▷Tell the story of Dürer's picture, on page 65.

▷Allow a few minutes for silent reflection.

▷Share your reactions to the story.

▷Draw around your hands on a piece of paper. Or, if you are able, draw your own picture of 'praying hands'. Compose a hand prayer that you can share with the group.

OUR WORLD

▶41
Using newspapers

1 Decide how long the idea is to last. This method of reflecting could be used on a daily basis or be a 'one off'. See how the group feels.

2 Obtain a selection of newspapers for that day.

3 Arrange for a small group to cut out events from the news that they would like to bring to the reflection time. This task could be given to different people each day.

4 Display a notice board or have an area which the group can see where they can display the cuttings.

5 Check that the items are balanced. You need positive, good news, as well as the more negative items.

▷Gather the group around the focal point.

▷Invite those who have prepared the day's reflection to introduce their items of news. They can either tell the group about them or read them out and then explain why they were chosen.

▷Allow the group time to talk about each of the items.

▷Spend a few moments thinking about what has just been said before moving on.

▷Light the candle.

▷If appropriate, a short response can be said between each piece of news, for example, 'Lord hear us . . . Lord graciously hear us', or 'In your mercy, Lord, hear our prayer'.

▷Display each of the items on the notice board or arrange them near the focal point.

▷Another variation on this idea is to allow each member of the group to pre-select an item of news and, in turn, share that with the group. All items are then displayed.

▶42
Using life stories

YOU WILL NEED:

1 A copy of your selected extract from a 'life story' for each member of the group. The extract does not need to be long. Try to select pieces that will challenge the reader to reflect on their own life.

2 Reflective music.

3 To invite members of the group to write a text or bring in one that means a lot to them.

4 A candle.

Life-story extracts

The following are two short extracts from true incidents in life which could form the basis for reflection and discussion.

Emma was a good laugh at school. Most people liked her. She'd liven up any lesson that was boring or in need of a bit of 'student participation', regardless of whether the teacher wanted it or not! She left school with the stamp of 'could have done better' written all over her leaver's report. In one final act of defiance, she tore up her school report and tossed it into the canal on the way home.

Emma rooted around in her pocket for her key, pulled out a box of matches, a few cigarette ends, sweet papers, notes with people's addresses hurriedly scribbled on them and half a packet of gum. The key was gone. Half wondering if she'd chucked the key into the canal with her report, Emma made her way past the bins, down through the back alley and into their tiny back yard. Suddenly Emma froze. The litter, the washing still on the line from three days ago, old shoes and wellies everywhere. Slowly Emma looked through the kitchen window. There sat her mum. Sitting where she'd sat for the past five years. Always in her dressing gown. Too sick to move more than a few agonizing paces at a time and too proud to allow anyone in to help. . . . Waiting for 'Our Em to come'. In a flash, the reality of what had happened that day hit Emma.

* * *

No one ever asked the old fellow where he lived. Come to think of it no one really knew whether his name was Jock or not. Jock was what he was called . . . By whom? Well, everyone who spoke to him. We'd see him every day with that little terrier of his on a bit of string. He'd come down to the village butcher, get a free bone for the dog, raise his hat in thanks and then make his way to the bench outside the village store. Great old boy he was. I heard many a tale about him in the War. I suppose, now that you mention it, I did notice him getting weaker in the winter. I often thought it must be cold out there on the bench. Made me glad to be inside my shop with a hot cuppa. Couldn't believe my ears when I heard that Marion's lad found him and that little dog frozen to death all wrapped up in cardboard. What on earth was he trying to do?

▷Gather the group in a semicircle around the focal point.

▷Light the candle.

▷Invite one of the group to read the chosen text. (Remember to prepare the text beforehand.) Or invite someone to tell their life story.

▷Allow a few minutes for personal reflection.

▷Invite the group to share their thoughts and feelings about the reading.

▷Share these with the group.

▷Play some reflective music and invite the group to be still and think about all that they have heard and shared that day.

▷Those who are keeping journals may like to write down their thoughts.

▶43
Using a calendar

YOU WILL NEED:

1 Calendars which indicate name days, special memorials, feast days or saints' days, or special times of the year.
The following agencies will help you with resources:

CAFOD, 2 Romero Close, Stockwell Road, London SW9 9TY.
The Thomas More Centre, The Burroughs, Hendon, London NW4 4TY.

2 To arrange the seating so that the whole group can see the calendar.

3 To invite a small group to prepare a short presentation on the day.

4 A candle.

5 A piece of paper for each member of the group and a pen.

▷ Gather the group around the calendar.

▷ Light the candle and place it near the calendar.

▷ Allow the presentation group time to explain what they are going to do.

▷ Talk about the aspect of the day that has been chosen, e.g. the saint, the name, the occasion or the feast.

▷ Invite each member of the group to spend a few minutes talking with a partner about the meaning of the day. What do special days like this do for the group? Do they have any effect at all? Are there things or people that they would like to see special days for?

▷ Gather up the thoughts of the group and ask them to think about keeping the memory of someone or some great event alive.

▷ Write down any great days, or special anniversaries that have occurred in their lives so far. Do they remember them? Why? How do they remember them? What do they do?

▷ If appropriate, spend the final few minutes talking about the importance of keeping special things alive in our memory by putting them on our own personal calendar.

►44
Using a map

YOU WILL NEED:

1 To invite one or two members of the group to select a country that they would like the group to think about. They should then gather some information on that country (one or two aspects to do with the way of life in that country) and make up an information sheet.

2 To find a large map of the world. Locate the chosen country beforehand.

3 Pins and string.

4 To discuss a method for identifying the chosen country on the map. This could be a small flag at the end of a pin marking the spot. A long piece of string could be attached which then runs to the side of the map, leading to the information sheet which the small group has prepared.

5 A small slip of paper and pen for each person to write down a couple of sentences.

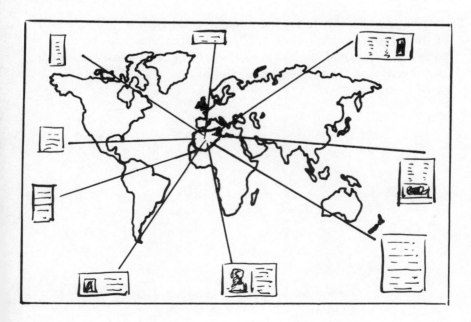

6 A candle.

7 To find a focal point where the map can be displayed for some time, especially if this idea is going to be used for several sessions.
(*This idea can be limited to a more local map or a map of the British Isles with students indicating towns, villages or streets.*)

▷Gather the group around the map.

▷Invite those who have prepared this reflection time to explain to the group what they are going to invite them to do.

▷Talk about the country of their choice: its people, their gifts, their needs and any special things that may be happening there.

▷As this is happening, mark the country with the pin. Pull the string, attached to the pin, to the edge of the map.

▷Invite each member of the group to write on a slip of paper one good wish for that country.

▷Light a candle and place it on the map beside the pin.

▷Ask each member of the group to read out their wish for that country.

▷As each person concludes their reading, they place it at the end of the string for that country. Place another pin through the pieces of paper and the loose end of string. The chosen country and the wishes for that country should now be linked by the piece of string.

THE TABLE

▶45
Using a table

YOU WILL NEED:

1 To invite a small group to help you with the preparations, as there is a lot to get ready for this idea.

2 A table large enough for everyone to sit around. This can be formed by moving several desks or smaller tables together. If this is not possible, you could sit the group into a large circle on the floor.

3 To invite each person to bring something that is very special to them to the session for that day. (Anything that can be put on the table or on the floor in the middle of the circle.)

4 To arrange the seating around the table.

5 To decorate the table with a cloth and candles and a Bible.

▷ Having prepared the table invite each member of the group to sit down around the table.

▷ In turn, ask each member of the group to place on the table the precious possession that they have brought and say something about it, e.g. how long they have had it, who gave it to them and why? What does it mean to them now? How would they feel if they lost it?

▷When everyone has spoken ask the group to spend a few minutes looking silently at all the different items on the table.

▷Play some background music quietly.

▷Think about the vast amount of love all those gifts represent. Each one very special and without a price because they are a symbol of love.

▷To conclude, read a few verses from 1 John 4:7–11.

▶46
Using meals

YOU WILL NEED:

1 To invite each person to bring something to eat for a special meal together.

2 To enlist the help of a small group to make the table look festive with flowers and candles.

3 To look in the Gospel accounts for times when Jesus had meals with his friends. Select storytellers from group members to familiarize themselves with these so that they can tell the story at the table. For example, stories like the feeding of the four and the five thousand, eating at Mary and Martha's house, the meal at Zacchaeus's house. The following are examples of some of the meals Jesus took part in:

Matthew 9:10–13	Luke 5:29–32	John 12:1–11
Matthew 14:13–21	Luke 10:38–42	John 13:1–20
Matthew 15:32–39	Luke 14:1–24	John 21:9–14
Matthew 26:6–13	Luke 24:36–43	
Matthew 26:17–19		
Matthew 26:26–29		

4 To select as many or few as the group thinks there will be time for.

5 To select some festive suitable music for the occasion.

▷ As the group gathers, play some festive music.

▷ Allow time for the helpers to arrange the food that each person has brought.

▷ When all is ready, everyone sits down to the table.

▷ Explain that Jesus always celebrated with his friends. As we read the Gospels, we see him time and time again going to people's houses to celebrate. He was often accused of mixing with the 'wrong company' and celebrating with them. Such was Jesus' love for every individual that he did not consider how bad they were or had been. If invited he would go.

▷ That is the purpose of the group's meal: celebrating, as Jesus did so often, through sharing food together.

▷ Everyone is then invited to eat from the table.

▷ At various times during the meal the group is invited to listen to a story – an account of an occasion when Jesus ate with his friends. As each person tells their story, the group is invited to share any thoughts that they may have about it.

▷ When everyone has finished eating, spend a few minutes saying 'thank you' to one another, thank you to those who prepared the celebration, and thank you to Jesus for the gift of one another and of himself.

Search for Meaning
Teacher's Book and Pupils' Worksheet Masters
SISTER JUDITH RUSSI

This new Sixth Form RE course is suitable for use with students of all beliefs and none. It has been successfully developed and piloted with large numbers of students over the past two years. The programme is divided into units of six sessions each: five of these are input sessions, the sixth a debate. This challenges students to study religious views and experiences and to defend their view-point in debate.

The Teacher's Book gives full details of how to run the two-year course and the worksheet photocopy masters provide a back-up for every session.

Sister Judith Russi SSMN is Schools' Officer and RE Adviser for the Hertfordshire area of Westminster diocese.

Teacher's Book   0 225 66607 3   192 pages
Worksheet Book   0 225 66608 1   A4   72 pages
Illustrations on every worksheet (worksheets are reproduced in book)

Life and Teaching of Jesus
GCSE Assignment Sheet Photocopy Masters

ANDREW LAWRENCE

These materials, provided in the form of photocopiable worksheets, can be used on their own with a Bible or in conjunction with a text book, to study the life and teaching of Jesus for GCSE.

▶ they are suitable for all syllabuses, take full account of GCSE Grade-related criteria and enable records of achievements to be built up

▶ contain a full range of mixed ability tasks, including tasks to challenge the more able

▶ illustrated throughout in a lively and thought-provoking style

▶ includes whole text of all Biblical passages needed

▶ self-supported study and individual learning are facilitated

▶ includes assessment sheets to help with Attainment Targets

▶ ideal for use in school or in Colleges of Further Education

▶ free of copyright to purchasing institution

Andrew Lawrence is head of Religious Studies at the Park School, Barnstaple, Devon.

0 264 67191 0   A4   96 pages   Illustrations on every page
Paperback   Mowbray   1990

Jesus in the Synoptic Gospels

DIANA MORGAN

Editorial Adviser: Edwin Cox

A 32 unit GCSE course based on study of St Mark's Gospel with cross references to the other Synoptic Gospels.

▶ Structured to encourage selection and presentation of factual information

▶ Designed to develop understanding of religious concepts and responses

▶ Students are encouraged to evaluate issues of belief and practice throughout

▶ Main text gives core information, with contextual background and extension material shown separately, to be used as required

▶ Test-Yourself and Check-Your-Understanding sections for revision/self-assessment

▶ Photographs selected to relate the Gospel narrative to life today

Diana Morgan is a retired Religious Education teacher.

Edwin Cox is a Senior Lecturer at the Institute of Education, University of London.

0 264 67031 0   96 pages   Black and white photographs
Paperback   Mowbray   1987